Easy Vegetarian Cooking:
75 Delicious Vegetarian Casserole Recipes

Gina 'The Veggie Goddess' Matthews

Copyright

Copyright © 2012 by Gina 'The Veggie Goddess' Matthews

Cover © Gina 'The Veggie Goddess' Matthews

All rights reserved. No part of this book may be reproduced in any form, or by any electronic or mechanical means, including information storage and retrieval systems – except in the case of brief quotations in articles or reviews – without the permission in writing from its publisher, Gina 'The Veggie Goddess' Matthews.

All brand names and product names used in this book are trademarks, registered trademarks, or trade names of their respective holders. The author is not associated with any product or vendor mentioned within this book.

ISBN: 148019297X
ISBN-13: 978-1480192973

DEDICATION

This book is dedicated to all those recognized and unrecognized kitchen goddesses, who infuse a little bit of love, into everything they cook.

TABLE OF CONTENTS

Dedication v
Table of Contents vii
Introduction 1
Chapter 1 – Veggie Based Casseroles 3
   Cinnamon Yam and Apple Casserole 5
   Cheesy Asparagus Casserole 6
   Baked Seasoned Vegetable Casserole 7
   Zesty Horseradish and Carrots Casserole 8
   Cheesy Smooth Broccoli and Onion Casserole 9
   Autumn Squash Casserole 11
   Velvety Corn and Chili Casserole 12
   Broccoli and Stuffing Casserole 13
   Creamy Cauliflower and Broccoli Casserole Bake 14
   Cinnamon Corn Bake 15
   Cream of Mushroom and Vegetable Casserole 16
   Spinach Souffle Casserole 17
   Zucchini Biscuit Casserole 19
   Grandma's Scalloped Corn Casserole 20
   Cheddar Broccoli Casserole 21
   Cornucopia Squash Casserole 22
   Root Vegetable Casserole 24
   Pumpkin Souffle' Casserole 25
   Cheddar Spinach Casserole 26
   Parmesan Cauliflower Casserole 27
   Cream of Mushroom Brussels Sprouts Casserole 28
   Cheddar Zucchini Casserole 29
   Eggplant Parmesan Casserole 30

Velvety Celery and Peppers Casserole...........32
Easy Creamy Squash Casserole...........33

Chapter 2 – Potato Based Casseroles...........35

Sweet Potato Souffle Casserole...........37
Hash Brown, Broccoli and Cheese Casserole...........38
Creamy Potato Souffle Casserole...........39
Tuscany Red Potatoes and Asparagus Casserole...........40
Smooth and Creamy Potato and Cauliflower Casserole.41
Potato and Jalapeno Au' Gratin Casserole...........43
Creamy Potato and Spinach Casserole...........44
Potato and Vegan 'Sausage' Casserole...........45
Tater Tot 'Helper' Casserole...........46
Sweet Potato, Apple and Fennel Casserole...........48
Cheddar Mashed Potato Casserole...........49
Autumn Spice Sweet Potato Casserole...........50
Hearty Vegetarian Sheppard's Pie Casserole...........52

Chapter 3 – 5 Ingredients or Less Spinach and Greens Recipes...........55

Seasoned Black Bean Casserole...........57
Taco Seasoned Bean Casserole...........58
Herb and Parmesan Green Bean Casserole...........59
Mediterranean Bean, Leek and Artichoke Casserole......60
Enchilada Bean Casserole...........62
Black Bean and Cornbread Casserole...........63
Creamy Green Bean Casserole...........65

Chapter 4 – Pasta Based Casseroles...........67

Cheesy Rotini and Veggie Casserole...........69
Cheddar Macaroni and Tomato Casserole...........70
Mac and Corn Casserole...........71
Tex Mex Pasta Casserole...........72
Stuffed Pasta Shells with Artichoke, Spinach and Feta...73
Cheesy Pasta and Beans Casserole...........75
Spinach, Mozzarella Pasta Casserole...........76

Chapter 5 – Rice Based Casseroles...........79

Simple and Savory Broccoli and Rice Casserole...........81
Wild Rice and Chiles Casserole...........82

Meatless Cabbage Rolls *83*
Simple Rice and Beans Casserole *86*
Brown Rice, Tofu and Vegetable Casserole *87*
Creamy Brown Rice and Cheese Casserole *88*
Wild and Brown Rice Vegetable Medley Casserole *90*
Elegant Brown Rice and Mushroom Casserole *91*
My Big Fat Greek Brown Rice Casserole *93*

Chapter 6 – Polenta, Hominy and Grits Based Casseroles 95

Roasted Red Pepper and Polenta Casserole *97*
Cheesy Baked Grits Casserole *98*
Cheesy Chile and Hominy Casserole *99*
Fajita Style Polenta and Vegetable Casserole *100*
Polenta and Soy 'Sausage' Casserole *102*
Rosemary Garlic Grits Casserole *103*
Taste of Italy Polenta Casserole *105*

Chapter 7 – Fruit Based Casseroles 107

Cran-Apple Streusel-Style Casserole *109*
Pineapple Cinnamon Casserole *110*
Spiked Basket of Fruit Casserole *111*
Peaches and Cream Casserole *112*
Apricot Casserole *113*
Autumn Fruit Casserole *114*
Brandied Banana Casserole *115*

Additional Books by Author 117
About The Author 119

INTRODUCTION

When you cook with love, people love what you cook. There is great fellowship, warmth and love, to be experienced around a dinner table, picnic, or potluck gathering. People come together over great food, and, people reach out to others through food. Because we experience through a multitude of senses, eating excites much more than just one's taste buds. Deliciously prepared food also brings pleasure through its eye-appealing presentations, wonderful aromas, and diverse textures.

Casseroles embody all of these wonderful qualities. And, at the same time, deliciously prepared casseroles, bring culinary and experience satisfaction to both those who prepare them, as well as to those who enjoy eating them.

The casserole recipes in this easy vegetarian cooking cookbook, offer both delicious and classic casserole creations, as well as creative, bold and exotic casserole creations. In this third book of 'The Veggie Goddess' vegetarian cookbook series, this expansive casserole recipe collection will help you find the perfect casserole recipe, for any meal, or event occasion.

These vegetarian recipes call for a 60/40 mix of fresh ingredients and packaged ingredients, making this vegetarian cookbook easy to follow for those who do not cook often, or who are not acclimated to using a lot of fresh vegetarian ingredients. For the more acclimated vegetarian, any of the prepared ingredients can be easily substituted with their fresh equivalent. Many of these recipes include dairy products, so, while not vegan, these ingredients can easily be swapped out with vegan ingredient substitutions.

Bon Veggie Appetit!

Gina 'The Veggie Goddess' Matthews

CHAPTER 1 – VEGGIE BASED CASSEROLES

You can enjoy all your favorite vegetables, from A-Z, with these mouth-watering, palate pleasing casseroles. From classic to creative, you'll find just what you're looking for, to bring to your next family or social gathering

Gina 'The Veggie Goddess' Matthews

Cinnamon Yam and Apple Casserole

(preheat oven to 350 degrees, and lightly grease a 2 quart casserole dish)

Ingredients:

2-3 large green apples (peeled, cored and diced)

3 large yams (peeled and cut into small diced-sized pieces)

½ cup water (divided)

½ cup of packed brown sugar

½ dark raisins

2 tablespoons butter (regular or vegan)

3 tablespoons flour (all-purpose)

¼ teaspoon ground cinnamon

¼ teaspoon sea salt

4-6 thin lemon slices

In a medium-sized pot over medium heat, mix together the butter, brown sugar, 1/3 cup of the water, raisins, cinnamon and sea salt. Stir continuously over medium heat, for 3-4 minutes, and then remove from heat. In a small mixing bowl, whisk together the flour, along with the remaining water, until well blended. Next, add the flour mixture into the seasoned brown sugar mixture, and stir well to blend.

Put the diced apple and yam pieces, into your prepared casserole dish. Hand toss to mix, and spread evenly in the baking dish. Next, evenly drizzle the brown sugar mixture across the top of the apples and yams, and top with the lemon slices. Cover with aluminum foil, and bake on center oven rack for 20 minutes. Uncover, and continue baking for an additional 20 minutes. Let dish stand for 5-7 minutes before serving. Yields 6-8 servings.

Cheesy Asparagus Casserole

(preheat oven to 350 degrees and lightly grease bottom of a 1-1/2 quart baking dish)

Ingredients:

1 can (15 ounce) asparagus (drained, and liquid reserved)

1 cup condensed cream of mushroom soup

2 cups crushed saltine crackers

1 cup Cheddar cheese (shredded)

½ cup butter (melted) – (regular or vegan)

½ cup almonds (pieces or slivers)

In a mixing bowl, stir together the melted butter, cream of mushroom soup and reserved asparagus liquid until blended. In a separate mixing bowl, stir together the crushed saltines with the shredded Cheddar cheese. Layer the bottom of your prepared baking dish with half of the Cheddar-cracker crumb mixture. Arrange half of the asparagus pieces on top of the crumb mixture, sprinkle with half of the almonds, and then half of the soup mixture. Add the other half of the asparagus, the other half of the soup mixture, and finish off with the remaining Cheddar crumb mixture. Bake for 20-25 minutes, or until top is golden brown. Yields 6-8 servings.

Baked Seasoned Vegetable Casserole

(preheat oven to 400 degrees, and lightly grease a large shallow baking dish)

Ingredients:

4 large zucchini (peeled and sliced into 1 inch rounds)

4 large carrots (peeled and cut into 1 inch rounds)

2 large potatoes, any variety (peeled and cubed)

1 head of broccoli (cored and cut into florets)

1 package (1 ounce) dry onion soup mix

¼ cup olive oil

Place all of your cut vegetables, into your prepared baking dish. Gently toss the vegetables to mix, and then add sea salt and pepper to taste. Drizzle the vegetables evenly with the olive oil, and then sprinkle with the dry onion soup mix. Bake for 40-45 minutes, or until vegetables or fork-tender. Yields 4-6 servings.

Zesty Horseradish and Carrots Casserole

(preheat oven to 350 degrees, and lightly grease the bottom of a 9x13 inch baking dish)

Ingredients:

1 package (16 ounce) frozen chopped carrots

½ cup cream (regular or light) – (regular or vegan)

3-1/2 tablespoons prepared horseradish

1 cup mayonnaise (regular or vegan)

2 tablespoons onion (finely diced)

¼ cup butter (melted) – (regular or vegan)

½ cup corn flake cereal (crushed)

Line prepared baking dish with the carrots. In a mixing bowl, whisk together the cream, horseradish, mayonnaise, onion and sea salt and pepper to taste. Once well blended, pour evenly across the carrots. In a small mixing bowl, stir together the melted butter and crushed corn flakes, and sprinkle evenly over the top of the casserole. Bake for 20 minutes, or until carrots are fork tender. Yields 6-8 servings.

Cheesy Smooth Broccoli and Onion Casserole

(preheat oven to 350 degrees, and lightly grease a 9x13 inch baking dish)

Ingredients:

3 heads of broccoli (cored and cut into florets)

4 yellow onions (rough chopped into somewhat large pieces)

1 package (8 ounce) cream cheese (room temperature) – (regular or vegan)

2 cups milk (regular or non-dairy)

8 ounces Cheddar cheese (shredded)

¼ cup butter (regular or vegan)

¼ cup flour (all-purpose)

¼ cup seasoned Italian bread crumbs

In a pot of salted water, steam the broccoli until just tender, about 5 minutes, and drain. In a separate pot, place the rough chopped onion with just enough water to cover, and bring to a low boil. Cook onions until just tender, and drain. Arrange the steamed broccoli and onion into your prepared baking dish. In a saucepan, over medium heat, melt the butter, and then whisk in the flour until smooth. Add in the milk, and continue cooking and stirring over medium heat, until sauce starts to thicken. Blend in the cream cheese, and add sea salt and pepper to taste. Cook and stir, until cream cheese is melted, and all ingredients are well blended. Pour mixture evenly over the broccoli and onions. Top with the shredded Cheddar cheese, and sprinkle with the seasoned bread crumbs. Cover with aluminum foil, and bake for 30 minutes. Remove the foil, and continue baking for an additional 30 minutes, or until top is a golden brown. Yields 10-12 servings.

Autumn Squash Casserole

(preheat oven to 325 degrees and lightly grease a 2 quart baking dish)

Ingredients:

3 cups cooked butternut squash (mashed)

½ cup of packed brown sugar

½ cup raw sugar

1 can (8 ounces) crushed pineapple (WITH juice)

¼ cup butter (melted) – (regular or vegan)

1 teaspoon ground cinnamon

1 teaspoon pure vanilla

1/8 teaspoon ground nutmeg

1/3-1/2 cup walnuts (finely chopped)

In a large mixing bowl, combine all ingredients EXCEPT for the walnuts. Stir well to blend, and then transfer into your prepared baking dish. Sprinkle top evenly with the chopped walnuts, and bake for 45 minutes. Yields 4-6 servings.

Velvety Corn and Chili Casserole

(preheat oven to 350 degrees and lightly grease a 8x8 baking dish)

Ingredients:

1 can (15.25 ounce) whole kernel corn (drained)

1 can (15.25 ounce) cream-style corn

1 can (4 ounce) chopped green chilies

2 packages (3 ounce each) cream cheese (softened room temperature) – (regular or vegan)

½ cup of diced red onion

¼ cup butter (softened to room temperature) – (regular or vegan)

1 package (2.8 ounce) French fried onions (divided)

2 teaspoons olive oil

Heat the oil in a small skillet, over medium heat. Add in the diced onion, sauté until translucent, about 3-4 minutes, and then immediately remove from heat. In a large mixing bowl, combine together, the softened butter and cream cheese. Once blended, stir in the whole kernel corn, cream-style corn, chilies and sautéed onions. Pour mixture in your prepared baking dish, and bake for 15 minutes. Remove from oven, and stir in half of the French fried onions. Re-spread evenly in baking dish, and sprinkle the remaining French-fried onions on top. Bake for an additional 15 minutes. Yields 6 servings.

Broccoli and Stuffing Casserole

(preheat oven to 350 degrees and lightly grease a 9x13 inch baking dish)

Ingredients:

2 pounds broccoli (cored and cut into florets)

1 large red onion (diced)

1 can (10.75 ounce) cream of mushroom soup

2 eggs (beaten)

½ cup mayonnaise (regular or vegan)

10 ounces of dry bread stuffing mix

½ cup butter (melted) – (regular or vegan)

1 cup Cheddar cheese (shredded)

In a pot of salted water, steam the broccoli until just tender, about 5 minutes, drain, and arrange the steamed broccoli into your prepared baking dish. In a mixing bowl, whisk together the beaten eggs, cream of mushroom soup, mayonnaise and diced onion. Once blended, spoon evenly over the broccoli, and add sea salt and pepper to taste. Spread the dry stuffing mix over the sauce, and then drizzle first with the melted butter, and lastly, the shredded Cheddar cheese. Bake on center oven rack for 30-35 minutes. Yields 10-12 servings.

Creamy Cauliflower and Broccoli Casserole Bake

(preheat oven to 425 degrees and lightly grease a 8x8 inch baking dish)

Ingredients:

6 ounces cauliflower florets

6 ounces broccoli florets

2-1/2 cups milk (regular or vegan)

2 tablespoons butter (regular or vegan)

2-1/2 tablespoons flour (all-purpose)

1 package (8 ounce) shredded sharp Cheddar cheese

1 teaspoon spicy brown mustard

pinch of cayenne

Steam the cauliflower and broccoli together in a large pot of salted water, until just fork tender, about 5 minutes. Drain, and arrange in your prepared baking dish. In a medium-sized saucepan, melt the butter over low-medium heat, and then whisk in the flour. Gradually add in the milk, while increasing heat to medium-high, while stirring frequently. Once mixture has started to thicken, whisk in the mustard, cayenne and sea salt and pepper to taste. Continue to stir frequently, being careful, to not allow mixture to come to a boil. Add in 2/3 of the shredded cheese, and stir until thoroughly melted. Pour the thickened sauce over the cauliflower and broccoli, and bake for 30 minutes. Top with the remaining shredded cheese, and bake for an additional 10 minutes. Let stand for 5 minutes, before serving. Yields 6-8 servings.

Cinnamon Corn Bake

(preheat oven to 350 degrees and lightly grease a 1-1/2 quart baking dish)

Ingredients:

2 cans (15 ounces each) whole kernel corn (drained)

2/3 cup evaporated milk

½ cup butter (regular or vegan)

3/4 cup sugar (divided)

¼ cup flour (all-purpose)

1 teaspoon ground cinnamon

Melt the butter in a large saucepan, over medium heat. Once melted, stir in ½ cup of the sugar. Next, whisk in the flour, until well blended, and remove saucepan from heat. Add in the evaporated milk and corn, and stir until all ingredients are well combined. Transfer mixture into your prepared baking dish, and bake for 60 minutes, or until a knife inserted into the center comes out clean. In a small mixing bowl, stir together the remaining ¼ cup sugar, along with the along cinnamon, and sprinkle over the top of the just bake casserole. Let stand for 5 minutes, before serving. Yields 4-5 servings.

Cream of Mushroom and Vegetable Casserole

(preheat oven to 350 degrees and lightly grease a 8x8 inch baking dish)

Ingredients:

1 package (16 ounce) frozen vegetable medley (broccoli, cauliflower and carrots)

1 can (10.75 ounce) cream of mushroom soup

1 cup shredded Cheddar cheese (divided)

1/3 cup sour cream (regular or light) – (regular or vegan)

1 package (2.8 ounce) French fried onions (divided)

Cook the frozen vegetables according to package directions, and drain. In a large mixing bowl, stir together the mushroom soup, ½ cup of the shredded cheese, sour cream, ½ of the French fried onions, and sea salt and pepper to taste. Once blended, stir in the cooked vegetables, and stir to blend. Transfer mixture to your prepared baking dish, and bake for 30 minutes. Remove from oven, top with the remaining shredded cheese and French fried onions, and bake for an additional 7-8 minutes. Yields 6 servings.

Spinach Souffle Casserole

(preheat oven to 350 degrees and lightly grease a 8x8 inch baking dish)

Ingredients:

3 packages (10 ounces each) of chopped frozen spinach (thawed and squeezed dry)

2 cups cottage cheese

3 eggs (beaten) – (may substitute with Ener-G egg replacer)

1-1/2 cup shredded Cheddar cheese (divided)

1/8 teaspoon ground nutmeg

In a large mixing bowl, mix together the cottage cheese and beaten eggs. Once blended, stir in the thawed, dried spinach (be sure ALL excess water has been removed), nutmeg, sea salt and pepper to taste, and 1-1/4 cups of the shredded cheese. Mix well, and be sure all ingredients are well blended before transferring to your prepared baking dish. Bake casserole on center oven rack for 45 minutes, or until soufflé is firm. Remove from oven, sprinkle top with the remaining shredded cheese, and let sit for 5-7 minutes before serving. Yields 8 servings.

Zucchini Biscuit Casserole

(preheat oven to 350 degrees and lightly grease a 9 inch pie plate)

Ingredients:

1 pound zucchini (ends trimmed and shredded with a grater or food processor)

1 small red onion (shredded with a grater or food processor)

1/3 cup buttermilk

½ cup grated Parmesan cheese (grated Romano cheese works well also)

1 cup biscuit baking mix

2 tablespoons olive oil

Combine all ingredients in a large mixing bowl, add sea salt and pepper to taste, and stir, until ingredients are well blended. Transfer mixture into your prepared pie plate, and bake for 1 hour, or until lightly browned. Let stand for 5minutes, before serving. Yields4-6 servings.

Grandma's Scalloped Corn Casserole

(preheat oven to 350 degrees, and lightly grease a 2 quart baking dish)

Ingredients:

3 cans (15 ounce each) cream-style corn

2 eggs (very lightly beaten)

1 cup crushed saltine crackers (divided)

½ cup butter (melted and divided) – (regular or vegan)

½ teaspoon paprika

In a mixing bowl, combine the corn, eggs, half of the melted butter (1/4 cup) and half of the crushed saltines (1/2 cup), and stir to blend. Pour mixture into prepared baking dish. Next, stir together the remaining melted butter and crushed saltines, along with the paprika, and sea salt and pepper to taste. Mixture should be crumbly. Sprinkle crumb mixture in an even layer on top of the corn, and bake for 35-40 minutes, or until top is bubbling around the edges. Let stand for 5 minutes before serving. Yields 8-10 servings.

Cheddar Broccoli Casserole

(preheat oven to 350 degrees and lightly grease a 9x13 inch baking dish)

Ingredients:

4 heads of broccoli (cored and cut into florets)

1 can (10.75 ounce) cream of mushroom soup

2 cups crushed seasoned breadcrumbs / croutons

1-1/2 cups shredded Cheddar cheese

3 tablespoons butter (regular or vegan)

In a pot of salted water, steam the broccoli until just fork tender, about 5 minutes, and drain. In a large saucepan over medium heat, combine the mushroom soup, shredded cheese, and sea salt and pepper to taste. Stir continuously, until cheese is melted. Add in the steamed broccoli, toss to coat, and transfer into your prepared baking dish. In a separate saucepan, melt the butter over medium heat. Once melted, add in the crushed breadcrumbs / croutons and stir to blend. Sprinkle evenly over the broccoli, and bake for 30-35 minutes, or until top is golden brown. Yields 8-10 servings.

Cornucopia Squash Casserole

(preheat oven to 350 degrees and lightly grease bottom only of a 9x13 inch baking dish)

Ingredients:

2 cups sliced yellow squash (only leave peels on if organic)

1 cup sliced zucchini squash (only leave peels on if organic)

1 yellow onion (diced)

2 large green onion spears (diced)

1 can (10.75 ounce) cream of mushroom soup

1 can (8 ounce) sliced water chestnuts (drained)

1 large carrot (shredded)

½ jar (4 ounce) diced pimento peppers (drained)

2 cups crushed Ritz-style crackers

½ cup butter (melted) – (regular or vegan)

½ cup mayonnaise (regular or vegan)

1 cup shredded sharp Cheddar cheese

2 cups water

1 teaspoon ground sage

½ teaspoon white or black pepper

1 teaspoon sea salt (divided)

In a large saucepan, combine the yellow squash, zucchini squash, yellow onion, green onion, water, and ½ teaspoon of the salt. Cook over medium heat for 7-8 minutes, and then drain. In a mixing bowl, stir together the melted butter and crushed crackers. Spread half of this mixture into the bottom of your prepared baking dish, and set the other half aside. Next, in a large mixing bowl, stir together the mushroom soup, mayonnaise, pimentos, carrots, water chestnuts, sage, pepper and remaining sea salt. Stir well, until all ingredients are well incorporated. Fold in the steamed squash into the mixture, and toss gently to blend. Spoon mixture across top of crust. Sprinkle with the shredded cheese, and top with the remaining half of the cracker crumb mixture. Bake for 30 minutes, then let stand for 5 minutes before serving. Yields 8 servings.

Root Vegetable Casserole

(preheat oven to 425 degrees and lightly grease a large, shallow baking dish or roasting pan)

Ingredients:

1 large rutabaga (peeled and cubed)

3 large red potatoes (peeled and cubed)

2 parsnips (peeled and cubed)

2 cups baby carrots

1 pound celery root (peeled and cubed)

2 red onions (cut into small wedges)

4 cloves of fresh garlic (cut into very thin slices)

1 cup vegetable broth

1-2 tablespoons olive oil

1 tablespoon fresh rosemary (diced)

In a large mixing bowl, combine all the ingredients EXCEPT the vegetable broth. Hand toss, to mix ingredients thoroughly. Transfer into your prepared baking dish or roasting pan, and bake for 30 minutes. Remove from oven, pour the vegetable broth over the veggies, and bake for an additional

20-25 minutes, or until the vegetables are fork tender. Yields 8 servings.

Pumpkin Souffle' Casserole

(preheat oven to 350 degrees and lightly grease the bottom only of a 2 quart baking dish)

Ingredients:

2 cups pumpkin puree (fresh or canned)

1 cup evaporated milk

1 cup sugar

½ cup flour (self-rising – do NOT use all-purpose)

2 eggs (very lightly beaten)

½ cup butter (softened, but NOT melted) – (regular or vegan)

1 teaspoon pure vanilla

pinch of ground cinnamon

pinch of ground nutmeg

Hand mix all the ingredients in a large mixing bowl, do not use a hand mixer. Once mixture is well blended, transfer into your baking dish, and bake on center oven rack for 60-65 minutes. Remove from oven, and let stand for 5 minutes before servings. Yields 8-10 servings.

Cheddar Spinach Casserole

(preheat oven to 350 degrees and lightly grease a 2 quart baking dish)

Ingredients:

1-1/4 pounds fresh spinach (washed, thoroughly dried and chopped)

3 eggs (beaten) – (may substitute with Ener-G egg replacer)

¼ cup butter (melted) – (regular or vegan)

1 cup milk (regular or non-dairy)

¾ shredded Cheddar cheese

½ cups crushed bread crumbs / croutons (plain or seasoned)

2 tablespoons fresh parsley (chopped)

¼ cup flour (all-purpose)

Arrange the spinach and flour in alternating layers

in your prepared baking dish, adding the eggs at the midpoint layer. In a mixing bowl, stir together the shredded cheese and crushed bread crumbs, add in the parsley, sea salt and pepper to taste, and sprinkle evenly over the spinach. Next, in a mixing bowl, whisk together the milk and melted butter. Pour evenly over casserole, and bake for 55-60 minutes. Let stand for 5 minutes before serving. Yields 8 servings.

Parmesan Cauliflower Casserole

(preheat oven to 375 degrees and lightly grease a 1-1/2 quart baking dish)

Ingredients:

1 large head of cauliflower (cored and cut into florets)

½ cup seasoned bread crumbs (or crushed seasoned croutons)

3 tablespoons grated Parmesan cheese (may substitute Romano cheese)

¼ cup butter (melted) – (regular or vegan)

1 clove fresh garlic (minced)

pinch of red pepper flakes (optional)

pinch of dried oregano

In a pot of salted water, steam the cauliflower until just fork tender, about 10-15 minutes, and drain. In a mixing bowl, combine the crushed bread crumbs / croutons, Parmesan cheese, and melted butter, and stir to blend. Next, add in the garlic, red pepper flakes, oregano, sea salt and pepper to taste, and mix well. Arrange the steamed cauliflower evenly into your prepared baking dish, and cover with the breadcrumb mixture. Bake for 15 minutes, or until golden brown. Yields 6-8 servings.

Cream of Mushroom Brussels Sprouts Casserole

(preheat oven to 350 degrees and lightly grease a 9x13 inch baking dish)

Ingredients:

2 packages (10 ounce each) frozen Brussels sprouts

1 can (10.75 ounce) cream of mushroom soup

2 eggs (beaten) – (may substitute with Ener-G egg replacer)

1 cup water

½ cup shredded Cheddar cheese

½ cup crushed bread crumbs or croutons, plain or seasoned (divided)

2 tablespoons butter (melted) – (regular or vega)

Cook the frozen Brussels sprouts according to package directions, and drain. In a mixing bowl, combine the melted butter, mushroom soup, eggs, shredded cheese, 1/3 cup of the bread crumbs, and sea salt and pepper to taste. Once blended, add in the steamed Brussels sprouts, and toss until evenly coated. Transfer into your prepared baking dish, and top with the remaining bread crumbs. Cover with aluminum foil, and bake for 25 minutes. Remove the foil, and bake for an additional 5 minutes. Let stand for 5 minutes before serving. Yields 6-8 servings.

Cheddar Zucchini Casserole

(preheat oven to 350 degrees and lightly grease a 9x13 inch baking dish)

Ingredients:

2 cups diced zucchini

4 thick slices stale bread (cubed)

1 small yellow onion (diced)

1 egg (beaten) – (may substitute with Ener-G egg replacer)

¼ cup butter (melted) – (regular or vegan)

2 cups shredded Cheddar cheese

1-2 cloves fresh garlic (minced)

Place the cubed stale bread in a mixing bowl, and slowly pour in the melted butter. Add in the diced zucchini, onion, garlic, egg, and sea salt and pepper to taste. Stir to blend, and then transfer into your prepared baking dish. Cover with aluminum foil, and bake for 30 minutes. Remove foil, and bake for an additional 30 minutes. Let stand for 5 minutes before serving. Yields 4 servings.

Eggplant Parmesan Casserole

(preheat oven to 350 degrees and lightly grease bottom of 2 quart baking dish)

Ingredients:

1 large eggplant (diced)

1 yellow squash (peeled and diced)

1 cup diced yellow onion

1 cup bread crumbs or crushed croutons (plain or seasoned)

1/8 cup diced green chiles

½ cup shredded mozzarella cheese

1 tablespoon butter (regular or vegan)

1/3 cup crushed Ritz-style crackers

Bring a large pot of salted water to a rolling boil. Add in the diced eggplant and squash, and cook until tender, but still firm, about 8-10 minutes. Drain, and let cool. In a large mixing bowl, combine the cooked, cooled eggplant and squash, onions, bread crumbs, butter and chiles. Stir well to blend, and then transfer into your prepared baking dish. Sprinkle with the crushed crackers, and top with the shredded cheese. Bake for 30 minutes. Let stand for 5 minutes before serving. Yields 4-6 servings.

Velvety Celery and Peppers Casserole

(preheat oven to 350 degrees and lightly grease bottom of 9x9 inch baking dish)

Ingredients:

4 cups thinly diced celery

4-5 large mushrooms (diced)

½ of a green bell pepper (diced)

1 jar (2 ounce) diced pimento peppers

6 tablespoon butter (divided) – (regular or vegan)

1 cup milk (regular or non-dairy)

1 cup shredded Cheddar cheese

3 tablespoons flour (all-purpose)

1 teaspoon sea salt

1 cup bread crumbs (plain or seasoned)

In a medium saucepan, melt 4 tablespoons of the butter over medium heat. Add in the celery, and cook until tender, about 5 minutes. Stir in the flour and sea salt, and blend until flour is fully dissolved. Next, pour in the milk, and continue to stir while cooking, until mixture starts to thicken. Once mixture has thickened, add in the mushrooms, green peppers, pimento peppers and shredded cheese, and stir until cheese has melted. Transfer mixture into your prepared baking dish. Melt the remaining 2 tablespoons of butter, and stir in the bread crumbs, to make a crumb mixture. Once blended, sprinkle the crumb mixture evenly across the top of the casserole, and bake for 25 minutes, or until top is lightly browned. Let stand for 5 minutes before serving. Yields 6 servings.

Easy Creamy Squash Casserole

(preheat oven to 350 degrees and lightly grease bottom of 9x9 inch baking dish)

Ingredients:

2 pounds yellow squash (peeled and cubed)

1 yellow onion (diced)

1 can (10.75 ounce) cream of mushroom soup

2 eggs (beaten) – (may substitute with Ener-G egg replacer)

2 cups shredded sharp Cheddar cheese

1-1/2 cups seasoned croutons

In a large pot of salted water, boil squash until tender, but still firm, about 10-15 minutes. Drain, and transfer into your prepared baking dish. In a mixing bowl, stir together the diced onion, soup, eggs and cheese. Once blended, pour evenly over the squash. Bake for 25 minutes. Remove from oven, layer with the seasoned croutons, and return to oven to bake for an additional 20 minutes. Let stand for 5 minutes before serving. Yields 6 servings.

CHAPTER 2 – POTATO BASED CASSEROLES

Potato lovers will delight, with this hearty and diverse potato casserole recipe selection. You're sure to win rave reviews from your family and friends, whenever you prepare these savory casseroles. Even the pickiest of eaters, won't be able to resist the aroma and taste of these delicious spud creations.

Gina 'The Veggie Goddess' Matthews

Sweet Potato Souffle Casserole

(preheat oven to 350 degrees and lightly grease bottom only of 2 quart baking dish)

Ingredients:

6 medium-large sized sweet potatoes

½ cup sugar

½ cup orange juice

½ cup of packed brown sugar

¼ cup flour (all-purpose)

¾ cup pecans (chopped)

½ teaspoon pure vanilla

3-1/2 tablespoons butter (divided) – (regular or vegan)

Bake your sweet potatoes in the oven, until well cooked. Allow sweet potatoes to cool, and then peel, rough chop, and place in a large mixing bowl. Mash the sweet potatoes together with the orange juice, 1-1/2 tablespoons of the butter, and sea salt to taste. Transfer to your prepared baking dish, and bake for 20 minutes. While dish is baking, combine the remaining ingredients in a mixing bowl, and stir to blend well. At the 20 minute baking mark, top the sweet potatoes off with the last layer of ingredients, and bake for an additional 25-30 minutes, keeping the oven door closed during entire cooking time. Let stand for 5 minutes before serving. Yields 6-8 servings.

Hash Brown, Broccoli and Cheese Casserole

(preheat oven to 350 degrees and lightly grease a 9x9 inch baking dish)

Ingredients:

1 package (12 ounce) frozen hash brown potatoes

1 package (12 ounce) frozen chopped broccoli

2 cups milk (regular or non-dairy)

1 package (3 ounce) cream cheese (diced) – (regular or vegan)

1/3 cup shredded Swiss, Monterey or Cheddar cheese

½ cup bread crumbs (plain or seasoned)

3 tablespoons butter (divided) – (regular or vegan)

2 tablespoons flour (all-purpose)

1 teaspoon sea salt

Melt 2 tablespoons of the butter in a saucepan, over medium heat. Once butter is melted, stir in the flour and sea salt. Add in the milk, and continue cooking and stirring, until mixture is bubbly. Add in the shredded cheese, and stir until cheese is melted. Next, add in the hash brown potatoes, and continue cooking until heated all the way through. Once thoroughly heated, line your prepared baking dish with half of the potato mixture. Cook the broccoli according to package directions, drain, and layer over the top of the potatoes. Cover the broccoli with the remaining potato mixture, sprinkle with the bread crumbs, and dot with the remaining 1 tablespoon of butter. Bake for 30-35 minutes, or until top is bubbly and golden brown. Let stand for 5 minutes before serving. Yields 8 servings.

Creamy Potato Souffle Casserole

(preheat oven to 325 degrees and lightly grease bottom of 1-1/2 quart baking dish)

Ingredients:

2 cups cooked mashed potatoes

1 package (8 ounce) cream cheese (softened to room temperature) – (regular or vegan)

2 eggs (beaten) – (may substitute with Ener-G egg replacer)

1 small yellow onion (diced)

1 tablespoon flour (all-purpose)

½ can (6 ounce) French fried onions

In a large mixing bowl, combine all ingredients EXCEPT for the French fried onions. Add sea salt and pepper to taste, and beat with an electric hand mixer for 2-3 minutes, at medium speed. Transfer mixture into your prepared baking dish, sprinkle the French fried onions evenly across the top, and bake for 35 minutes. Yields 2 servings.

Tuscany Red Potatoes and Asparagus Casserole

(preheat oven to 425 degrees and lightly grease bottom of 2 quart baking dish)

Ingredients:

1-1/2 pounds red potatoes (cubed)…..only leave the skin on, if organic

1 bunch asparagus (ends trimmed and diced)

4 cloves fresh garlic (minced)

2-3 sprigs fresh rosemary (chopped)….may substitute 4 teaspoons dried rosemary

2-3 sprigs fresh thyme (chopped)....may substitute 4 teaspoons dried thyme

4 tablespoons olive oil (divided)

2 teaspoons sea salt

Arrange the diced potatoes in your baking dish, along with 2 tablespoons of the olive oil, half of the rosemary, half of the thyme, and half the sea salt. Cover with aluminum foil, and bake for 20 minutes. Remove from oven, and stir in the diced asparagus, and remaining olive oil, rosemary, thyme and salt. Recover and bake for an additional 15 minutes. Next, remove foil, INCREASE oven temperature to 450 degrees, and bake for a final 10 more minutes. Yields 6 servings.

Smooth and Creamy Potato and Cauliflower Casserole

(preheat oven to 350 degrees and lightly grease bottom of 2 quart baking dish)

Ingredients:

2 extra large golden potatoes (peeled and cubed)

1 head cauliflower (cored and cut into florets)

3 tablespoons butter (regular or vegan)

3 tablespoons flour (all-purpose)

1 cup heavy cream (do NOT substitute with milk or half-n-half)

1 cup shredded Swiss cheese (divided)

In a pot of salted water, boil the cubed potatoes until tender but still firm, about 5-8 minutes, drain, and set aside. In a large covered pot, steam the cauliflower florets until just fork tender about 5 minutes, drain and set aside. Melt the butter in a medium-sized saucepan over medium heat. Whisk in the flour, and then gradually add in the heavy cream, whisking and cooking over medium heat, until sauce starts to thicken. Remove from heat, and stir in ½ cup of the Swiss cheese until melted, and add sea salt and pepper to taste. Arrange the cooked potatoes and cauliflower into your prepared baking dish, and toss gently to mix. Pour the cream sauce evenly over the top, and sprinkle with the remaining ½ cup of Swiss cheese. Bake 20-25 minutes, or until top is lightly browned and bubbly. Yields 4-6 servings.

Potato and Jalapeno Au' Gratin Casserole

(preheat oven to 350 degrees and lightly grease a 9x13 inch baking dish)

Ingredients:

2 pounds of golden potatoes (peeled and sliced into 1/8 inch round slices)

2 cups shredded Gruyere cheese

3 large jalapeno peppers (seeded and diced)

2 cups heavy whipping cream

1 tablespoon paprika

Spread ¼ of the potato slices along the bottom of your prepared baking dish. Layer with 1/3 of the shredded cheese, followed by 1/3 of the diced jalapeno. Sprinkle with sea salt and pepper to taste, and then repeat the layers 2 more times…potato slices – cheese – jalapeno – seasoning. Next, gently pour the heavy cream evenly over the top of the casserole, and sprinkle with the paprika. Bake for 1-1/2 hours (90 minutes). Let stand for 5 minutes before serving. Yields 6-8 servings.

Creamy Potato and Spinach Casserole

(preheat oven to 400 degrees and lightly grease bottom of 2 quart baking dish)

Ingredients:

7 large russet potatoes (peeled and cubed)

1 package (10 ounce) frozen spinach (thawed and well drained)

1 cup sour cream (regular or light)

¼ cup butter (softened) – (regular or vegan)

2-3 tablespoons diced green onions

2 teaspoons sea salt

¼ teaspoon ground black pepper

1 cup shredded Cheddar cheese

In a large pot of salted boiling water, cook cubed potatoes until fully tender, about 7-8 minutes, drain, and transfer into a large mixing bowl. Hand mash the potatoes thoroughly, and then stir in all the remaining ingredients EXCEPT the cheese. Stir to blend, add sea salt and pepper to taste, and then transfer mixture into your prepared baking dish. Bake for 15 minutes. Remove from oven, top with the shredded cheese, and bake for an additional 5-8 minutes, until cheese is melted and bubbly. Let stand for 5 minutes before serving. Yields 8 servings.

Potato and Vegan 'Sausage' Casserole

(preheat oven to 350 degrees and lightly grease bottom of 9x13 inch baking dish)

Ingredients:

5 red or golden potatoes (peeled and cubed)

1 package (12 ounce) vegan sausage (cut into ½ inch rounds)....try 'Tofurky Kielbasa'

1 yellow onion (diced)

4 tablespoons butter (regular or vegan)

2-1/2 cups milk (regular or non-dairy)

3 broccoli crowns (diced)

1-2 cloves fresh garlic (minced)

1 package (8 ounce) shredded Monterey jack cheese

4 tablespoons flour (all-purpose)

4 tablespoons crushed bread crumbs (plain or seasoned)

Boil the cubed potatoes, mock sausage, and onion, in a covered pot with 2 inches of water, until potatoes are just fork tender. Drain, and set aside. Melt the butter in a saucepan, over medium heat. Add in the garlic and sauté for 1-2 minutes. Whisk in the flour, and then gradually add in the milk, whisking continuously while cooking. Once the sauce starts to thicken slightly, add in the shredded cheese, and sea salt and pepper to taste. Once cheese has melted, remove saucepan from heat. Arrange the cooked potatoes, mock sausage and onion mixture evenly into your prepared baking dish. Pour the sauce evenly over the top, and then add the diced broccoli. Sprinkle the breadcrumbs across the top, and then bake for 50-60 minutes. Casserole is done when bubbly, and forms a crust on top. Let stand for 5 minutes before serving. Yields 6-8 servings.

Tater Tot 'Helper' Casserole

(preheat oven to 400 degrees and lightly grease bottom of 9x13 inch baking dish)

Ingredients:

1 package (28 ounce) frozen tater tots

1 package (12 ounce) frozen meatless crumbles

8 ounces mushrooms (diced)

1 yellow onion (diced)

2 cups vegetable broth

½ cup sour cream

1 packet (1.8 ounce) dry onion soup mix

1 tablespoon corn starch

1 tablespoon soy sauce

1-2 cloves fresh garlic (minced)

4 ounces French fried onions

1 package (8 ounces) shredded Cheddar cheese

2-3 tablespoons olive oil

Heat the oil in a large skillet, over medium heat. Add in the onions and sauté until translucent. Stir in the mushrooms and sauté for another 2 minutes. Add in the frozen meatless crumbles, garlic, soy sauce and sea salt and pepper to taste. Heat the mixture, until the meatless crumbles are heated through, and then remove from heat. Transfer the mixture into your prepared baking dish, and top with the frozen tater tots. In a medium saucepan, combine the vegetable broth, dry soup mix, sour cream and cornstarch. Bring to a boil, immediately reduce heat to medium-low, and simmer until sauce starts to thicken, while continuously stirring. Once sauce has thickened, pour evenly over the tater tots.

Top with a layer of French fried onions, followed by the shredded cheese, and bake for 35-40 minutes. Let stand for 5 minutes before serving. Yields 6-8 servings.

Sweet Potato, Apple and Fennel Casserole

(preheat oven to 400 degrees and lightly grease bottom of 8x8 inch baking dish)

Ingredients:

3 large sweet potatoes (peeled and thinly sliced)

2 green apples (peeled, cored and thinly sliced)

1 large fennel bulb (thinly sliced)

1 large onion (cut into thin rings)

2 tablespoons soy sauce

1 tablespoon hoisin sauce

1 tablespoon cornstarch (OR potato starch)

½ teaspoon ground cumin

½ teaspoon cayenne pepper

1-2 tablespoons real maple syrup, grade 'A' or 'B' (do NOT use pancake syrup)

1 packet stevia

½ cup cold water

In a mixing bowl, whisk together the soy sauce, hoisin, cumin, cayenne, maple syrup and stevia with the ½ cup of cold water, and then add in the cornstarch. (You can add up to ¾ cup of water if needed.) You want the sauce to be slightly thick, and not runny. Arrange the cut sweet potatoes, apples, fennel and onion, into your prepared baking dish, and toss gently to mix. Drizzle evenly with half of the sauce, cover with aluminum foil, and bake for 30 minutes. Remove from oven, uncover, and drizzle the remaining sauce over the top (give the sauce a quick stir, before pouring). Bake uncovered for an additional 30-40 minutes, or until sweet potatoes are fork tender. Yields 4 servings.

Cheddar Mashed Potato Casserole

(preheat oven to 350 degrees and lightly grease bottom of 9x9 inch baking dish)

Ingredients:

1 package (22 ounce) frozen mashed potatoes

2 large eggs (beaten) – (may substitute with Ener-G egg replacer)

1 small package (3 ounce) cream cheese (softened)

1 small yellow onion (diced)

1 jar (2 ounce) diced pimento (UN-drained)

1 cup shredded sharp Cheddar cheese

Prepare the frozen mashed potatoes according to package directions, adding sea salt and pepper to taste. Once the potatoes are cooked, fold in the eggs, softened cream cheese, onion and pimento. Transfer mixture into your prepared baking dish, cover with aluminum foil, and bake for 30 minutes. Remove from oven, remove the foil, and top with the shredded cheese. Bake for an additional 10-12 minutes, and then let stand for 5 minutes before serving. Yields 6 servings.

Autumn Spice Sweet Potato Casserole

(preheat oven to 350 degrees and lightly grease bottom of a 2 quart baking dish)

Ingredients:

6 large sweet potatoes (cooked, peeled and mashed)

¼ cup evaporated milk

1 teaspoon pure vanilla

¼ cup orange juice

½ cup sugar

½ teaspoon sea salt

3 tablespoons butter (melted) – (regular or vegan)

½ teaspoon ground nutmeg

½ teaspoon ground cinnamon

Ingredients of Topping:

1/3 cup butter (melted) – (regular or vegan)

¾ cup of packed brown sugar

½ cup flour (all-purpose)

¾ cup finely crushed pecans

In a large mixing bowl, combine the mashed sweet potatoes, evaporated milk, orange juice, vanilla, sugar, sea salt, 3 tablespoons of the melted butter, nutmeg and cinnamon. Stir by hand, or use a manual hand mixer, and blend thoroughly. Transfer mixture into your prepared baking dish. Next, you'll prepare the topping, by hand mixing together the 1/3 cup melted butter, brown sugar, flour and crushed pecans. Sprinkle the topping mixture evenly over the top of the casserole, and bake for 45-50 minutes. Let stand for 5 minutes before serving. Yields 6 servings.

Hearty Vegetarian Sheppard's Pie Casserole

(preheat oven to 375 degrees and lightly grease bottom of a large baking dish)

Ingredients:

1 cup small diced carrots

½ cup small chopped broccoli

½ cup small chopped cauliflower

½ cup green beans (small rough chopped)

½ cup peas

½ cup small chopped mushrooms

4 tablespoons butter (divided) – (regular or vegan)

¼ cup flour (all-purpose)

1 cup vegetable broth

2/3 cup milk (regular or non-dairy)

2 tablespoons chopped fresh sage

4 large potatoes (peeled and diced)

¼ cup plain yogurt (regular or non-dairy)

½ cup fresh grated Parmesan cheese

In a covered pot, steam all the cut vegetables together (EXCEPT the potatoes), until just fork tender. Drain, and return vegetables to the pot. Add in 2 tablespoons of the butter, flour, vegetable broth, milk and sage. Cook and stir over medium heat, until mixture starts to thicken. Stir in sea salt and pepper to taste, and remove from heat. Boil the cut potatoes in a pot of salted water, until tender. Drain, and mash in a bowl, together with the yogurt and Parmesan cheese. Spread the cooked vegetables in your prepared baking dish, and top with an even spreading of the potatoes. Bake for 35-40 minutes, and let stand for 5 minutes before serving. Yields 4-6 servings.

Gina 'The Veggie Goddess' Matthews

CHAPTER 3 – 5 INGREDIENTS OR LESS SPINACH AND GREENS RECIPES

Beans are nature's great protein-carbohydrate balanced food. And, with a little culinary creativity, they are anything but the boring food staple, that many people associate beans to be. Satisfying your hunger, taste buds and weight control, beans are little food gems can be the backbone of some incredibly delicious casserole creations.

Gina 'The Veggie Goddess' Matthews

Seasoned Black Bean Casserole

(preheat oven to 350 degrees and lightly grease bottom of 3 quart baking dish)

Ingredients:

1 pound dry black beans

1-1/2 cup diced red onion

4 cloves fresh garlic (minced)

3 large celery stalks (diced)

2 large carrots (peeled, and cut into thin rounds)

2 fresh bay leaves

1 tablespoon fresh chopped parsley or cilantro

4 tablespoons butter (regular or vegan)

¼ teaspoon dried oregano

Give the beans a thorough rinse, and then transfer them into a large pot of water, and bring to a full boil, over medium heat. Once water boils, cover pot, remove from heat, and let stand for 1 hour. After 1 hour, drain the beans, rinse a second time, and return them to the pot and cover with fresh water. Add in all the remaining ingredients, EXCEPT for the butter. Bring to a boil, reduce heat, cover, and simmer for 2 hours on low heat. Be sure to stir mixture regularly. Next, remove the bay leaves, stir in the butter, and transfer into your prepared baking dish. Cover with aluminum foil, and bake for 1 hour. Let stand for 5 minutes before serving. Yields 8 servings.

Taco Seasoned Bean Casserole

(preheat oven to 350 degrees and lightly grease bottom of 9x13 inch baking dish)

Ingredients:

2 cans (15.5 ounce each) kidney beans (drained)

2 cans (10.75 ounce) condensed tomato soup

2 cups fresh corn (may also use frozen/thawed or canned/drained)

2 cups corn chips (crushed)

1-1/2 cups shredded Cheddar cheese

1 packet taco seasoning (or, add in your own taco seasoning spice combination)

In a large mixing bowl, combine the beans, soup, corn and taco seasoning. Stir well, until all ingredients are well blended. Transfer into your prepared baking dish, layer with the crushed corn chips, and top with the shredded cheese. Bake for 30-35 minutes. Yields 6 servings.

Herb and Parmesan Green Bean Casserole

(preheat oven to 350 degrees and lightly grease bottom of 8x8 inch baking dish)

Ingredients:

2 cans (14 ounce each) regular or French cut green beans (drained)

¾ cup plain or seasoned breadcrumbs (divided)

1 cup freshly grated Parmesan cheese (freshly grated vs. container cheese makes a BIG difference in taste with this dish)

2 cloves fresh garlic (minced)

1 teaspoon dried oregano

2 teaspoons dried parsley

2 teaspoons dried basil

½ teaspoon dried thyme

½ cup olive oil

In a large mixing bowl, stir together the breadcrumbs, grated Parmesan, all the spices, and sea salt and pepper to taste. Once blended, set aside 2-3 tablespoons of the crumb mixture, to use as a topping. Next, add in the drained green beans and olive oil, and stir well to evenly coat. Transfer into your prepared baking dish, and sprinkle the reserved crumb mixture evenly over the top. Bake for 30 minutes, or until top is crispy and golden brown. Yields 4-6 servings.

Mediterranean Bean, Leek and Artichoke Casserole

(preheat oven to 400 degrees and lightly grease bottom of 9x9 inch baking dish)

Ingredients:

1 cup seasoned breadcrumbs

2 cans (15 ounce each) navy beans (liquid RESERVED)

½ teaspoon dried thyme

½ teaspoon dried sage

¼ teaspoon black pepper

3 cloves fresh garlic (minced)

3 tablespoons olive oil (divided)

3 cups chopped leeks (about 3 large)

½ teaspoon dried rosemary

¼ teaspoon sea salt

1 can (14 ounce) artichoke bottoms (drained and chopped)

1-1/4 cup crumbled goat cheese

Drain beans over a bowl, reserving the liquid. Add enough water to the reserved liquid, to measure 1 cup, and set aside. In a mixing bowl, stir together the drained beans, thyme, sage, garlic and black pepper, and set aside. Heat 2 tablespoons of the olive oil in a skillet, over medium heat. Add in the garlic, leeks, rosemary, sea salt and artichokes, and sauté for 5 minutes. Pour in the 1 cup of bean liquid (not the bean mixture), cover, reduce heat to low, and simmer for 10-12 minutes. Remove from heat. Spread half of the bean-spice mixture into the bottom of your prepared baking dish, and top with half of the goat cheese. Next, add the artichoke mixture over the layer of goat cheese, followed by the remaining half of the bean mixture, and remaining half of the goat cheese. Sprinkle top with the breadcrumbs, and drizzle with the remaining 1 tablespoon of olive oil. Bake for 25-30 minutes. Let stand for 5 minutes before serving. Yields 4-6 servings.

Enchilada Bean Casserole

(preheat oven to 350 degrees and lightly grease bottom of 9x13 inch baking dish)

Ingredients:

2 cans (15.8 ounce each) black beans (drained)

2 cups diced red onion

2 cups diced red peppers

2-3 cloves fresh garlic (minced)

¾ cup salsa

2 teaspoons ground cumin

12 corn tortillas (6 inch size)

2 cups shredded Monterey cheese (divided)

3 large tomatoes (diced)

½ cup sliced black olive

½ cup sour cream

In a skillet over medium heat, sauté the drained beans, salsa, onion, garlic, onion and peppers for 4-5 minutes, and then remove from heat. Line your prepared baking dish with a layer of 6 corn tortillas, and then spread half of the bean mixture over the top. Sprinkle with 1 cup of the shredded cheese, and then make another layer…6 corn tortillas, remaining half of bean mixture, remaining half of shredded cheese. Cover with aluminum foil, and bake for 20 minutes. Let stand for 5 minutes before serving. Sprinkle top with the sliced olives and tomatoes, and serve with the sour cream on the side. Yields 8 servings.

Black Bean and Cornbread Casserole

(preheat oven to 350 degrees and lightly grease bottom of 8x8 inch baking dish)

Ingredients for filling:

½ can (15.8 ounce) black beans (drained)

1 cup corn (may also use frozen/thawed or canned/drained)

2 cloves fresh garlic (minced)

1-1/2 tablespoon olive oil

¾ cup diced red onion

1 tomato (diced)

½ teaspoon chili powder

½ teaspoon ground cumin

Ingredients for top layer:

½ cup yellow cornmeal

½ cup flour (all-purpose)

1-1/2 teaspoons baking powder (aluminum-free)

½ tablespoon sugar

2 tablespoons butter (softened to room temperature) – (regular or vegan)

½ teaspoon sea salt

2/3 cup coconut milk

Heat the 1-1/2 tablespoons olive oil in a skillet, over medium heat. Add in the onion and garlic, and sauté for 3 minutes. Add the diced tomato, sea salt, chili powder and cumin, and stir continuously while cooking for another 3-4 minutes. Add the drained beans and corn, and cook for 3 more minutes, before removing from heat, and transferring mixture into your prepared baking dish. In a mixing bowl, stir together the cornmeal, flour, baking powder and sugar. Add in the softened butter and coconut milk, and whisk until smooth. It should have a spreadable consistency. Carefully spread the batter with a spatula over the bean mixture, and then bake uncovered for 30 minutes. Let stand for 5 minutes before serving. Yields 6 servings.

Creamy Green Bean Casserole

(preheat oven to broil and lightly grease bottom of 8x8 inch baking dish)

Ingredients:

1 pound fresh green beans (ends trimmed and rough chopped)

1 small yellow onion (cut into thin half rings)

1-2 tablespoons fresh chopped parsley

3 tablespoons butter (softened and divided) – (regular or vegan)

2 tablespoons flour (all-purpose)

½ teaspoon of fresh lemon zest (use the lemon afterwards to squeeze on top after cooked)

½ teaspoon sea salt

¼ teaspoon ground black pepper

½ cup milk (regular or non-dairy)

1 cup sour cream

½ cup shredded Cheddar or Monterey cheese

¼ cup fine breadcrumbs (plain or seasoned)

Steam the green beans in a pot of salted water, until just crisp-tender. Drain, and set aside. Heat 2 tablespoons of the butter in a saucepan, over medium heat. Add in the onion and chopped parsley, and cook until onion becomes translucent, about 4 minutes. Whisk in the flour, lemon zest, sea salt and pepper. Once the flour is dissolved, add in the milk, and cook while whisking continuously until mixture starts to thicken and become bubbly. Add in the sour cream and cooked green beans, and heat until mixture again begins to bubble. Remove from heat, spoon mixture into your prepared baking dish, and layer with the shredded cheese. Melt the remaining 1 tablespoon butter, and stir in the breadcrumbs. Sprinkle the crumb mixture evenly across top of casserole, and broil (set your oven rack about 5 inches from broiler) until cheese is melted and slightly browned, about 3-5 minutes. Let stand for 5 minutes before serving. Yields 4-6 servings.

CHAPTER 4 – PASTA BASED CASSEROLES

High on the comfort food list for vegetarians and non-vegetarians alike, pasta is an incredibly versatile food ingredient to work with. Enjoy the following vegetarian pasta casserole recipes, and may they inspire you to create your very own signature veggie pasta dish.

Gina 'The Veggie Goddess' Matthews

Cheesy Rotini and Veggie Casserole

(preheat oven to 375 degrees and lightly grease bottom of 3 quart baking dish)

Ingredients:

1 package (8 ounce) rotini pasta

1 package (20 ounce) frozen mixed vegetables of your choice

1 can (10.75 ounce) tomato soup

1 cup sour cream (regular or light)

2 cups shredded Cheddar cheese (divided)

1-2 tablespoons diced yellow onion

Prepare both the rotini and frozen vegetables according to package directions, and drain. In a large mixing bowl, combine the cooked rotini, vegetables, tomato soup, sour cream, diced onion, and 1 cup of the shredded cheese. Stir well to blend. Transfer into your prepared baking dish, and top with the remaining 1 cup of shredded cheese. Bake for 35-40 minutes. Let stand for 5minutes before serving. Yields 8 servings.

Cheddar Macaroni and Tomato Casserole

(preheat oven to 350 degrees and lightly grease bottom of 9x13 inch baking dish)

Ingredients:

1 pound of macaroni pasta (you may substitute with spiral, elbow or other small pasta shape)

1 can (10.75 ounce) condensed tomato soup

1-1/4 cup milk (regular or non-dairy)

3 cups shredded Cheddar cheese (may substitute with mozzarella cheese)

8 tablespoons butter (softened and divided) – (regular or vegan)

¼ cup crushed bread crumbs or croutons

Cook the pasta according to package al dente' directions, and drain. In a large mixing bowl, combine the cooked pasta with the soup, milk, cheese, and 6 tablespoons of the softened butter. Transfer into your prepared baking dish. Top evenly with crushed bread crumbs, and dot with the remaining 2 tablespoons of softened butter. Bake for 45 minutes. Let stand for 5 minutes before serving. Yields 6 servings.

Mac and Corn Casserole

(preheat oven to 350 degrees and grease bottom of 8x8 baking dish)

Ingredients:

1 can (11.25 ounce) whole kernel corn (drained)

1 can (14.75 ounce) cream-style corn

1 cup dry macaroni pasta

8 ounces shredded Cheddar or Colby cheese

½ cup butter (softened) – (regular or vegan)

In a large mixing bowl, stir together both of the corns, with the uncooked macaroni. Add in the softened butter and shredded cheese, and mix well. Transfer into your prepared baking dish, cover with aluminum foil, and bake for 30 minutes. Remove the foil, stir, and bake for an additional 30 minutes. Let stand for 5 minutes before serving. Yields 6 servings.

Tex Mex Pasta Casserole

(preheat oven to 350 degrees and lightly grease bottom of 9x13 inch baking dish)

Ingredients:

2 cups pasta (spiral, penne, elbow or macaroni style)

1 can vegetarian chili

1 can (15.5 ounce) kidney beans (drained)

1 large tomato (diced)

¼ cups diced green chiles

½ cup corn

1 cup chopped spinach leaves

¾ cup peas

¾ cup diced mushrooms

pinch of red pepper flakes

1 package (8 ounce) shredded Monterey cheese

Cook pasta according to package directions, drain, and set aside. In a large mixing bowl, combine all remaining ingredients, EXCEPT the cheese. Once ingredients are well blended, fold in the cooked pasta, and add sea salt and pepper to taste. Transfer into your prepared baking dish, top with the shredded cheese, and bake for 30 minutes. Let stand for 5 minutes before serving. Yields 4-6 servings.

Stuffed Pasta Shells with Artichoke, Spinach and Feta

(preheat oven to 375 degrees and lightly grease bottom of 9x13 inch baking pan)

Ingredients:

20 cooked jumbo shell pasta

1 package (9 ounce) frozen artichoke hearts (thawed and chopped)

½ of a package (10 ounce – you'll use 5 ounces worth) frozen spinach (thawed, squeezed dry and chopped)

1 can or jar (28 ounce) of fire-roasted crushed tomatoes with added puree

1 can (8 ounce) tomato sauce

¼ cup diced pepperoncini peppers

1 cup shredded provolone cheese (divided)

1 cup crumbled feta cheese

4 ounces cream cheese (softened)….this is half of a package

2 cloves fresh garlic (minced)

1 teaspoon dried oregano

¼ teaspoon ground black pepper

In a medium saucepan over medium heat, combine the fire-roasted tomatoes, tomato sauce, diced pepperoncinis, and oregano. Cook for 10-12 minutes, until sauce starts to thicken. Remove from heat and set aside. In a large mixing bowl, combine ½ cup of the shredded provolone, the feta cheese, softened cream cheese, chopped artichokes, chopped spinach, and garlic, and blend thoroughly. Spoon or pipe about 1-1/2 tablespoon of cheese mixture into each cooked pasta shells, and place them into the baking dish in a single layer. Pour the tomato sauce mixture evenly over all the stuffed shells, and top with the remaining ½ cup shredded provolone. Bake for 25-30 minutes. Let stand for 5 minutes before serving. Yields 4-5 servings.

Cheesy Pasta and Beans Casserole

(preheat oven to 375 degrees and lightly grease bottom of 2 quart baking dish)

Ingredients:

1 package (16 ounce) penne pasta (or any other small shaped pasta)

1 can (14.5 ounce) diced tomatoes

2 cans (16 ounce each) kidney beans (drained, and rinsed to remove starch)

1 jar (26 ounce) of your favorite spaghetti sauce

2 cloves fresh garlic (minced)

2 cups shredded mozzarella cheese

Prepare pasta according to package directions, drain, and return to saucepan. Stir in all the remaining ingredients, EXCEPT the cheese. Mix well to blend, and then transfer to your prepared baking dish. Top with the shredded cheese, and bake for 40 minutes. Let stand for 5 minutes before serving. Yields 4-6 servings.

Spinach, Mozzarella Pasta Casserole

(preheat oven to 375 degrees and lightly grease bottom of 9x13 inch baking dish)

Ingredients:

¾ pound small shaped pasta (shells, macaroni, elbows, spirals, etc.)

3 tablespoons olive oil (divided)

1 large red onion (diced)

2 cloves fresh garlic (minced)

4 cups fresh spinach (well chopped)

1-1/2 cups almond slivers (divided)

zest of 2 lemons (divided)

8 ounces shredded mozzarella cheese

Prepare pasta according to package directions. Drain, and then toss with 1 tablespoon of the olive oil, in a mixing bowl. Heat the remaining 2 tablespoons of olive oil in a large skillet, over medium heat. Add in the onion and garlic, and sauté for several minutes, until the onions become translucent. If you want to caramelize your onions, toss in a pinch of sea salt when sautéing. Turn off heat, and toss in the spinach. Stir the spinach constantly for about 30 seconds (just long enough for the spinach to wilt), and then spoon into the mixing bowl with your cooled pasta. Add in 1 cup of the almonds, and the zest from 1 of the lemons. Toss well for about 1 minute, until ingredients are well blended. Sprinkle the bottom of your prepared baking dish with the zest of the remaining lemon. Spoon in half of the pasta mixture, layer with half of the shredded cheese, followed by the remaining half of the pasta, and the remaining half of the cheese. Cover with aluminum foil, and bake for 30 minutes. Remove from oven, sprinkle top with the remaining ½ cup almonds, and let stand for 5 minutes before serving. Yields 6 servings.

Gina 'The Veggie Goddess' Matthews

CHAPTER 5 – RICE BASED CASSEROLES

One of the best ways to use leftover rice, is to create a little casserole magic. Throw in some extra ingredients, and you have the makings of a hearty, flavor-rich dish the whole family will love.

Gina 'The Veggie Goddess' Matthews

Simple and Savory Broccoli and Rice Casserole

(preheat oven to 325 degrees and lightly grease bottom only of 8x8 inch baking dish)

Ingredients:

1 package wild rice mix

2 heads of broccoli (cored, and cut into florets)

1 can cream of mushroom soup

2 cups shredded Cheddar cheese

Prepare the wild rice according to package directions. Layer the cooked rice into the bottom of your prepared baking dish. Steam the broccoli until just fork tender, about 5 minutes, and drain, and spread the steamed broccoli over the rice. In a mixing bowl, stir together the mushroom soup and cheese, and then pour evenly on top of casserole. Bake for 50-55 minutes. Let stand for 5 minutes before serving. Yields 6 servings.

Wild Rice and Chiles Casserole

(preheat oven to 325 degrees and lightly grease bottom of 8x8 baking dish)

Ingredients:

1 package (6 ounce) instant long grain and wild rice mix

1 container (8 ounce) sour cream (regular or light)

1 can (4 ounce) chopped green chiles

1 package (16 ounce) shredded Cheddar cheese

Prepare the rice according to package directions. Once cooked, spread half of the rice into the bottom of your prepared baking dish. In a mixing bowl, mix together the sour cream and green chiles. Spread half of the mixture over the layer of rice, and then sprinkle with half of the shredded cheese. Repeat the layers…rice – sour cream mixture – cheese, and then bake for 25-30 minutes. Let stand for 5 minutes before serving. Yields 4-6 servings.

Meatless Cabbage Rolls

(preheat oven to 375 degrees and lightly grease bottom of 9x13 inch baking dish)

Ingredients for Rolls:

2 heads of green cabbage

¾ cup uncooked white rice

1-1/4 cup textured soy protein

1-1/4 cup vegetable broth

4 tablespoons butter (regular or vegan)

1 large yellow onion (diced)

3 tablespoons Worcestershire sauce

1 tablespoon soy sauce

1-2 cloves fresh garlic (minced)

1 egg (beaten) – (may substitute with Ener-G egg replacer)

Ingredients for Sauce:

1 can (28 ounce) diced tomatoes

2 tablespoons butter (regular or vegan)

2 tablespoons flour (all-purpose)

1 clove fresh garlic (minced)

½ cup vegetable broth

½ teaspoon dried thyme

½ teaspoon sugar

2 tablespoons tomato paste

4 tablespoons fresh parsley (chopped)

Halve and core the 2 heads of cabbage, and boil them in a large pot of salted water for 10-15 minutes. Drain, and allow cabbage to cool. Boil the rice in salted water for 10 minutes, or until ALMOST tender. Drain, rinse, and allow rice to cool.

Re-hydrate the textured soy protein, using the 1-1/4 cups of vegetable broth. In a skillet over medium heat, saute the onion in the 4 tablespoons of butter, until softened. Stir in the textured soy protein, and cook for 3-5 minutes. Next, mix in the Worcestershire sauce, soy sauce, garlic and sea salt and pepper to taste. Once blended, remove from heat.

In a large mixing bowl, combine together the textured soy protein mixture, with the rice and beaten egg, making sure all ingredients are well blended. Separate the cooled cooked cabbage leaves, and lay them out on a clean work surface. Divide the cabbage filling evenly amongst all the leaves, placing the filling directly in the center of each leaf. Next, roll your filled cabbage leaves up, folding the sides in around the filling and then rolling from the thick end towards the thin end.

Arrange your cabbage rolls tightly together into your baking dish. Depending on how many rolls you have, you may need to create an extra layer or two on top of each other. Next, pour enough water into your baking dish, so that it comes halfway up the sides of your dish. Cover tightly with aluminum foil, and bake for 30 minutes.

While the rolls are baking, melt the 2 tablespoons of butter in a medium-sized saucepan over medium heat, and then whisk in the flour. Cook for 1 minute, and then add in the diced tomatoes, tomato paste, ½ cup vegetable broth, garlic, thyme, sugar and sea salt and pepper to taste. Bring to a boil while stirring continuously, then cover, reduce heat, and cook on low for 20 minutes. Break up the diced tomatoes with a fork, as the sauce cooks.

Remove your rolls from the oven, and carefully drain all but a very shallow layer of water from your baking dish. You can either pour it out, or use a baster. Pour your sauce evenly over your rolls, and then return to oven, and cook uncovered for an additional 20-25 minutes. Let stand for 5 minutes before serving. Sprinkle with the fresh parsley before eating. Yields 8-10 servings.

Simple Rice and Beans Casserole

(preheat oven to 350 degrees and lightly grease bottom of 2 quart baking dish)

Ingredients:

1 can (28 ounce) vegetarian baked beans

1-1/2 cups cooked rice (a great way to use leftover rice)

½ cup diced red onion

½ cup shredded carrots

½ cup thinly diced celery

1 clove fresh garlic (minced)

¼ teaspoon cinnamon

1/8 teaspoon ground ginger

Combine all the ingredients in a large mixing bowl, and stir well to blend. Transfer into your prepared baking dish, and bake for 40 minutes. Let stand for 5 minutes before serving. Yields 4-6 servings.

Brown Rice, Tofu and Vegetable Casserole

(preheat oven to 350 degrees and lightly grease bottom of 2 quart baking dish)

Ingredients:

2 cups cooked brown rice

1 package (12 ounce) extra firm tofu (drained and diced)

3 slices of sprouted grain or whole wheat bread (cut into cubes)

4-1/2 tablespoons olive oil

2 tablespoons butter (regular or vegan)

½ cup diced yellow onion

1 cup milk (regular or non-dairy)

2 tablespoons soy sauce or Tamari sauce

1 cup Cheddar or mozzarella cheese (cubed)

½ cup grated Parmesan or Romano cheese

1 cup cooked chopped broccoli

With your cooked rice set aside, heat the olive oil in

a large skillet, over medium heat. Add in the onion and sauté for 4-5 minutes. Stir in the tofu, cooked rice, broccoli and soy sauce. Remove from heat, and gently fold in the cubed bread, and cubed cheese. Pour in the milk, and gently stir, until all ingredients are well blended. Transfer into your prepared baking dish, sprinkle with the grated cheese, and bake for 50-60 minutes. Let stand for 5 minutes before serving. Yields 4 servings.

Creamy Brown Rice and Cheese Casserole

(preheat oven to 350 degrees and grease bottom of 9x13 inch baking dish)

Ingredients:

3 cups cooked brown rice (cooled to room temperature)

2 large eggs (may substitute with Ener-G egg replacer)

1 cup cottage cheese

½ cup sour cream

1 teaspoon spicy brown mustard

½ teaspoon sea salt

1-1/2 tablespoons olive oil

8 ounces crimini mushrooms (diced)

1 large yellow onion (diced)

3 cloves fresh garlic (minced)

1 cup grated Gruyere cheese (divided)

1 teaspoon fresh chopped tarragon

In a large mixing bowl, whisk together the eggs, cottage cheese, sour cream, mustard and sea salt. Once blended, set mixture aside. Heat the olive oil in skillet, over medium heat. Add in the diced mushrooms, along with a couple pinches of sea salt, and sauté for 5 minutes. Stir in the diced onion, and continue stirring and cooking, until onions become translucent. Next, add in the minced garlic and cooled rice, and stir well, to blend all ingredients. Spoon rice mixture into the mixing bowl with the egg mixture, and fold, until all ingredients are well blended. Transfer into your prepared baking dish, sprinkle with ½ cup of the shredded cheese, and cover tightly with aluminum foil. Bake for 30 minutes. Remove the foil, and bake for an additional 30 minutes, adding the remaining ½ cup of shredded cheese during the last 10 minutes of cooking. Let stand for 5 minutes, garnish with the chopped tarragon, and serve. Yields 6-8 servings.

Wild and Brown Rice Vegetable Medley Casserole

(preheat oven to 350 degrees and lightly grease bottom of 2 quart baking dish)

Ingredients:

1 cup uncooked brown rice

½ cup uncooked wild rice

1 large red bell pepper (diced)

1 large green bell pepper (diced)

1 zucchini (diced)

1 large carrot (peeled and cut into thin slices)

1 large celery stalk (diced)

2 cloves fresh garlic (minced)

2 cups vegetable broth

2 tablespoons butter (softened to room temperature) – (regular or vegan)

Rinse the brown and wild rice, and put into a large mixing bowl. Stir in the red pepper, green pepper, zucchini, carrot, celery, garlic, butter, and sea salt and pepper to taste. Once all the ingredients are well mixed, transfer into your prepared baking dish, and pour the vegetable broth over the top. Cover tightly with aluminum foil, and bake for 30 minutes. Check if more water needs to be added, and bake for an additional 15-30 minutes, or until rice is tender. Yields 4 servings.

Elegant Brown Rice and Mushroom Casserole

(preheat oven to 350 degrees and lightly grease bottom of 9x9 inch baking dish)

Ingredients:

3 cups cooked brown rice (cooled to room temperature)

8 ounces any variety mushroom (diced)

2 tablespoons olive oil

1 large yellow onion (diced)

2-3 cloves fresh garlic (minced)

2 large eggs (may substitute with Ener-G egg replacer)

1 cup cottage cheese

½ cup sour cream

½ teaspoon sea salt

½ cup fresh grated Parmesan cheese (divided)

1 tablespoon of fresh chopped tarragon

Heat the olive oil in a large skillet, over medium heat. Add in the diced mushrooms, along with a big pinch of sea salt, and sauté until mushrooms have started to brown. Add in the diced onion, and sauté for another 5 minutes, or until onions become translucent. Stir in the garlic, and cook for 1 more minute, before removing from heat. Fold the rice into the mushroom mixture, and set aside. In a large mixing bowl, whisk together the eggs, cottage cheese, sour cream and sea salt. Pour the rice mixture into your bowl with the cream mixture, stir well to blend, and transfer into your prepared baking dish. Sprinkle top with ¼ cup of the grated Parmesan, cover with aluminum foil, and bake for 30 minutes. Remove the foil, and bake for an additional 20-30 minutes, or until the sides are golden brown. Sprinkle with the chopped tarragon, and remaining ¼ cup Parmesan cheese, and let stand for 5 minutes before serving. Yields 6-8 servings.

My Big Fat Greek Brown Rice Casserole

(preheat oven to 375 and lightly grease bottom of 9x9 inch baking dish)

Ingredients:

4 cups cooked brown rice (cooled to room temperature)

2 tablespoons olive oil

1 large yellow onion (diced)

1-1/2 large red peppers (top sliced off and diced)

2 cloves fresh garlic (minced)

2 teaspoons Greek seasoning blend (Penzeys is a good brand)

6-8 ounces crumbled feta cheese (plain or seasoned)

¼ cup vegetable broth

Heat the olive oil in a large saucepan, over medium heat. Add in the onion and garlic, and sauté for 4-5 minutes, or until onions become translucent. Stir in the red peppers and seasoning, and sauté for an additional 3 minutes. Add in the cooked rice, and stir continuously while cooking, for another 2-3 minutes. Remove from heat, and gently fold in the feta crumbles and vegetable broth. Transfer into your prepared baking dish, cover with aluminum foil, and bake for 25 minutes. Remove the foil, and bake for an additional 10 minutes. Let stand for 5 minutes before serving. Yields 6-8 servings.

CHAPTER 6 – POLENTA, HOMINY AND GRITS BASED CASSEROLES

Most people wouldn't even think that they can create a taste-satisfying dish using polenta, hominy or grits. Well, prepare to be surprised. Just as versatile as potatoes, pasta and rice, these three base ingredients easily absorb the flavors of the other ingredients they are prepared with, and therefore, they can satisfy a wide range of taste preferences.

Gina 'The Veggie Goddess' Matthews

Roasted Red Pepper and Polenta Casserole

(preheat oven to 350 degrees and lightly grease a 9x9 inch baking dish)

Ingredients:

½ tube of pre-made polenta (thinly sliced)

1/3 cup shredded carrots

1 large tomato (top sliced off and cut into thin slices)

¼ cup extra-firm tofu (freeze – defrost – and then crumble)

¼ cup frozen spinach (thawed and all excess water squeezed out)

1 sprig fresh rosemary (diced)

1 teaspoon dried basil

1-1/2 roasted red peppers (seeded and rough chopped)

½ cup crushed saltines

2 tablespoons butter (melted) – (regular or vegan)

Line the bottom of your prepared baking dish with

the polenta slices, overlapping as needed. Sprinkle evenly with sea salt and pepper to taste. Spread the shredded carrots over the layer of polenta. Next, top with a layer of tomato slices, and sprinkle evenly with the basil. In a mixing bowl, mix together the frozen tofu crumbles, spinach, and chopped rosemary. Spread crumb mixture evenly over top of the tomato layer. Lay the red pepper pieces across the top, and sprinkle with the crushed saltines. Carefully drizzle the melted butter over the top, and cover with aluminum foil. Bake for 20 minutes, remove foil, and bake for an additional 10 minutes. Let stand for 5 minutes before serving. Yields 4-6 servings.

Cheesy Baked Grits Casserole

(preheat oven to 350 degrees and lightly grease bottom of 2 quart baking dish)

Ingredients:

1 cup uncooked grits

1 quart milk (regular or non-dairy)

½ cup butter + 1/3 cup butter (regular or vegan)

1 cup shredded Cheddar cheese

½ cup grated Parmesan cheese

In a saucepan over medium heat, bring the milk to a boil. Melt in the ½ cup of butter, into the boiling milk. Slowly add in the grits, and cook while stirring for 5 minutes. Remove from heat, and add in sea salt and pepper to taste. Next, beat mixture with either a whisk, hand mixer, or electric mixer, until smooth and creamy. Stir in the Cheddar cheese, and the remaining 1/3 cup of butter. Transfer into your prepared baking dish, and sprinkle top with the Parmesan cheese. Bake for 60 minutes. Let stand for 5 minutes before serving. Yields 10 servings.

Cheesy Chile and Hominy Casserole

(preheat oven to 350 degrees and grease bottom of 2 quart baking dish)

Ingredients:

2 cans (15.5 ounce each) white hominy (drained)

1 can (7 ounce) chopped green chiles (drained)

1 package (8 ounce) cream cheese (softened) – (regular or vegan)

2 cloves fresh garlic (minced)

½ cup diced yellow onion

½ cup shredded Cheddar OR Colby cheese

1 tablespoon olive oil

Heat the olive oil in a skillet, over medium heat. Add in the diced onion and garlic, and sauté until soft, and slightly translucent in color. Reduce heat to medium-low, and stir in the green chiles, and softened cream cheese. Continue cooking and stirring, until cream cheese is melted. Remove from heat, and stir in the shredded cheese, hominy and added sea salt and pepper to taste. Transfer into your prepared baking dish, and bake for 35-40 minutes. Let stand for 5 minutes before serving. Yields 6-8 servings.

Fajita Style Polenta and Vegetable Casserole

(preheat oven to 350 degrees and lightly grease bottom of 9x13 inch baking dish)

Ingredients:

1 tube (16 ounce) polenta (sliced into 1/2 " rounds)

1 can (15 ounce) kidney beans (drained)

1 can (16 ounce) black beans (drained)

1 can (10 ounce) whole kernel corn (drained)

6 large mushrooms (diced)

1 small eggplant (peeled and cubed)

1 large green pepper (diced)

1 large red onion (diced)

1/3 cup pitted black olives (thinly sliced)

1 packet (1.27 ounce) fajita seasoning (or use your own blend of fajita spices)

3 tablespoons olive oil

1 cup shredded mozzarella cheese

1 jar (8 ounce) salsa

Heat the oil in a large skillet, over medium heat. Add in the onion, green pepper, eggplant and mushrooms, and sauté until vegetables are tender, but still firm. Stir in fajita seasoning, mix well, and remove from heat. Line your prepared baking dish with the polenta slices, overlapping as needed. Spread the drained beans and corn evenly over the polenta layer, and then top with the seasoned sautéed vegetables. Top with a layer of salsa, mozzarella cheese, and finally the black olives. Bake for 25-30 minutes. Let stand for 5 minutes before serving. Yields 6 servings.

Polenta and Soy 'Sausage' Casserole

(preheat oven to 350 degrees and grease bottom of 8x8 inch baking dish)

Ingredients:

1 tube polenta, sliced into 1 inch slices (plain or sun dried tomato)

1 package of 'Soyrizo' sausage

1 can (16 ounce) black beans (drained)

1 small red onion (diced)

1 large tomato (diced)

2 tablespoons olive oil

1 package (8 ounce) shredded Mexican-style cheese

Heat the oil in a medium saucepan, over medium heat. Squeeze the Soyrizo out of the tube into the pan, along with the onions. Cook for 5 minutes, while breaking up the Soyrizo with a spatula. Add in the black beans and diced tomatoes, reduce heat to low, and cook for 8-10 minutes, to allow flavors to build. Layer the bottom of your prepared baking dish with the polenta slices, overlapping as needed. Spoon the Soyrizo mixture over the polenta, and then sprinkle the cheese evenly over the top. Cover with aluminum foil, and bake for 25 minutes. Let stand for 5 minutes before serving. Yields 4 servings.

Rosemary Garlic Grits Casserole

(preheat oven to 400 degrees and lightly grease bottom of 11x7 inch baking dish)

Ingredients:

1 cup seasoned breadcrumbs

½ cup grated Parmesan cheese

3 tablespoons fresh chopped parsley

7 cups boiling water (divided)

3 ounces sun dried tomatoes (diced)

1 tablespoon olive oil

2 cups thin sliced red onion

1 tablespoon fresh chopped rosemary

1/8 teaspoon crushed red pepper

2 cloves fresh garlic (minced)

1-1/2 teaspoon sea salt (divided)

1 can (19 ounce) any variety of white beans

(drained)

1-1/2 cup uncooked grits

2 tablespoons butter (regular or vegan)

In a large bowl, combine 3 cups of the freshly boiled water with the sun dried tomatoes, and let stand for 10 minutes. Once tomatoes have softened, drain over a bowl, and reserve 1 cup of the liquid. Heat the olive oil in a skillet, over medium heat, and add in the onion, rosemary, crushed red pepper and garlic, and sauté for 3-4 minutes. Add in the tomatoes and reserved 1 cup liquid. Bring to a boil, and cook for 7-9 minutes, or until most of the liquid evaporates. Stir in the drained beans, and add sea salt and pepper to taste. Once blended, remove from heat.

In a large saucepan, combine the remaining 4 cups of boiling water with 1 teaspoon of the salt, the grits, and 2 tablespoons of butter. Cook for about 8 minutes over medium heat, while stirring continuously. Transfer cooked grits into your prepared baking dish, top with tomato mixture, followed by the seasoned breadcrumbs. Bake for 20-25 minutes. Let stand for 5 minutes before serving. Yields 6 servings.

Taste of Italy Polenta Casserole

(preheat oven to 400 degrees and lightly grease bottom of 9x13 inch baking dish)

Ingredients:

2 tablespoons olive oil

2 cups diced red onion

3 cups chopped cremini mushrooms (12 ounces)

1-1/2 teaspoons sea salt (divided)

2 cloves fresh garlic (minced)

1/3 cup dry red wine

1 tablespoon chopped fresh rosemary (may substitute with 1 teaspoon dried)

1 tablespoon tomato paste

1 can (14.5 ounce) diced tomatoes (KEEP the liquid)

4 cups water

1 cup instant polenta (such as Contadina)

½ cup FRESH grated Parmesan cheese (divided)

1/8 teaspoon ground black pepper

½ cup ricotta cheese

2-3 teaspoons butter (regular or vegan)

Heat the olive oil in a skillet, over medium heat. Add in the onion and sauté for 5 minutes. Stir in the mushrooms, ½ teaspoon of the sea salt and garlic, and cook for another 4-5 minutes. Add in the wine, rosemary and tomato paste. Once the tomato paste starts to become thinned, add the diced tomatoes with their liquid, and cook until mixture starts to thicken, about 10-12 minutes. Once thickened, remove from heat.

In a saucepan, bring the 4 cups of water to a boil, and stir in the polenta, along with the remaining 1 teaspoon of sea salt. Reduce heat to low, and cook until thickened, about 5-7 minutes, making sure to stir frequently. Once cooked, spread 1/3 of the polenta into the bottom of your baking dish. Pour ½ of the tomato sauce over the top, and sprinkle evenly with 2 tablespoons of the grated Parmesan, and the 1/8 teaspoon of black pepper. Dot the ricotta cheese evenly over the layer of Parmesan, and then repeat the layers….polenta – sauce – Parmesan – ricotta. Top with a final layer of polenta and sprinkle of cheese. Finally, dot the butter over the layered casserole, and bake for 25-30 minutes. Let stand for 5 minutes before serving. Yields 6 servings.

CHAPTER 7 – FRUIT BASED CASSEROLES

Everyone naturally craves something sweet, to one degree or another. These sweet fruit casserole dishes are easy to prepare, and guaranteed crowd pleasers. Whether served for breakfast, brunch, a baby or wedding shower, or to bring along to a potluck, people will gobble up these sweet, delicious treats fast.

Gina 'The Veggie Goddess' Matthews

Cran-Apple Streusel-Style Casserole

(preheat oven to 350 degrees)

Ingredients:

1 can (16 ounce) whole berry cranberry sauce

1 can (21 ounce) apple pie filling

1-1/2 cups rolled oats

¾ cup packed brown sugar

¼ cup butter (softened to room temperature) – (regular or vegan)

Combine the cranberry sauce and apple pie filling in a shallow baking dish, and stir to blend. In a mixing bowl, mix together the softened butter, rolled oats and brown sugar, until crumbly. Sprinkle the streusel topping over top of fruit, and bake for 35-40 minutes, or until top is crisp and browned. Yields 6 servings.

Pineapple Cinnamon Casserole

(preheat oven to 350 degrees and lightly grease bottom of a 8x8 inch baking dish)

Ingredients:

1 can (20 ounce) crushed pineapple WITH the juice
5 pieces of white bread (hand torn into small pieces)
4 eggs (may substitute with Ener-G egg replacer)
1 cup sugar
½ cup butter (softened) – (regular or vegan)
pinch of ground cinnamon
pinch of ground nutmeg

In a mixing bowl, cream together the butter and sugar, with a hand mixer. Beat in the eggs, one at a time. Once the mixture is smooth and creamy, hand stir in the cinnamon and nutmeg, followed by the bread pieces, and the pineapple with juice. Transfer into your prepared baking dish, and bake for 1 hour. Let stand for 5 minutes before serving. Yields 4-6 servings.

Spiked Basket of Fruit Casserole

(preheat oven to 300 degrees and lightly grease bottom of large baking dish)

Ingredients:

1 can (28 ounce) peach halves (drained)

1 can (28 ounce) pear halves (drained)

1 can (15 ounce) chunk pineapple (drained)

1 can (17 ounce) apricot halves (drained)

1 can (17 ounce) dark pitted cherries (drained)

1 can (17 ounce) Kadota figs

1 bag sweetened shredded coconut

3 large bananas (peeled and cut into ½ inch slices)

½ cup almonds (slivers or pieces)

1/3 cup packed brown sugar

2/3 cup banana liqueur OR amaretto liqueur

½ of a large lemon

In a large mixing bowl, stir together all your drained fruit, banana slices, figs and liqueur. Line your prepared baking dish with the entire package of shredded coconut, and then layer your fruit mix evenly on top of the coconut. Squeeze the ½ of a lemon evenly over your fruit, being careful not to let any seeds fall into the dish. In a small mixing bowl, stir together the brown sugar and almond pieces, and sprinkle the mixture across the top of your casserole. Bake for 40 minutes. Yields 10 servings.

Peaches and Cream Casserole

(preheat oven to 350 degrees and lightly grease bottom of 8x8 inch baking dish)

Ingredients:

1-3/4 cups peaches (peeled and thinly sliced)

¼ cup sugar

1-1/2 cup rolled oats

2 egg whites

2 teaspoons almond extract

3 cups milk (regular or non-dairy)

In a large mixing bowl, stir together the sliced peaches, sugar and oats. In a separate mixing bowl, whisk together the egg whites, almond extract and milk. Pour the liquid mixture into the oat mixture, and stir well to blend all ingredients. Transfer into your prepared baking dish, and bake for 50-55 minutes. Let stand for 5 minutes before serving. Yields 4-6 servings.

Apricot Casserole

(preheat oven to 350 degrees and lightly grease bottom of 8x8 inch baking dish)

Ingredients:

1 can (17 ounce) apricot halves (drained)

½ cup sugar

1 full stack (1 tube package) Ritz-style crackers (crushed)

4 tablespoons butter (regular or vegan)

Arrange the apricot halves into the bottom of your prepared baking dish. In a mixing bowl, stir together the sugar and crushed crackers, and sprinkle over the apricots. Dot the top evenly with the butter, and bake for 30-35 minutes. Yields 4 servings.

Autumn Fruit Casserole

(preheat oven to 375 degrees and lightly grease bottom of 3 quart baking dish)

Ingredients:

6 medium carrots (peeled and cut into ½ inch slices)

3 sweet potatoes (peeled and cubed)

2 large green apples (peeled, cored and diced)

¼ pound pitted prunes (chopped)

¼ pound apricots (peeled and diced)

2 tablespoons raw honey

1 teaspoon ground cinnamon

½ teaspoon ground nutmeg

½ teaspoon sea salt

1 cup orange juice

2 tablespoons butter (regular or vegan)

Boil, or steam, the carrots and sweet potatoes, until just fork tender, about 5-8 minutes. Drain, and transfer into a large mixing bowl. Stir in all the remaining ingredients, EXCEPT for the butter. Once blended, transfer mixture into your prepared baking dish, and bake for 45 minutes, stirring once every 15 minutes. Remove from oven, dot with the 2 tablespoons of butter, and bake for an additional 10-15 minutes. Let stand 5 minutes before serving. Yields 6 servings.

Brandied Banana Casserole

(preheat oven to 350 degrees and lightly grease bottom of 9x13 inch baking dish)

Ingredients:

6 large bananas (peeled and halved lengthwise)…you should have 12 halved banana pieces

½ cup of packed brown sugar

½ cup butter (diced into small pieces) – (regular or vegan)

½ cup chopped pecans

½ cup dark raisins

3 tablespoons brandy

Line the bottom of your prepared baking dish with half of the banana slices (6). Sprinkle evenly with half the brown sugar (1/4 cup), half of the diced butter pieces, half the chopped pecans (1/4 cup), and half the raisins (1/4 cup). Repeat with a second layer - 6 remaining banana slices, the remaining half of the brown sugar, the remaining half of the pecans, and the remaining half of the raisins. Bake for 30 minutes. Remove from oven, drizzle the brandy across top of casserole, and let stand for 5-10 minutes, before serving. Yields 6 servings.

ADDITIONAL BOOKS BY AUTHOR

- Easy Vegetarian Cooking: 100 – 5 Ingredients or Less, Easy & Delicious Vegetarian Recipes
- Easy Vegetarian Cooking: 75 Delicious Vegetarian Soup and Stews Recipes
- Natural Foods: 100 – 5 Ingredients or Less, Raw Food Recipes for Every Meal Occasion
- The Veggie Goddess Vegetarian Cookbook Collection: Volumes 1-4
- Easy Vegan Cooking: 100 Easy & Delicious Vegan Recipes
- Vegan Desserts: 50 Delectable Vegan Dessert Recipes
- Holiday Vegan Recipes: Holiday Menu Planning for Halloween through New Years
- The Veggie Goddess Vegan Cookbooks Collection: Volumes 1-3

- Natural Cures: 200 All Natural Fruit & Veggie Remedies for Weight Loss, Health and Beauty

ABOUT THE AUTHOR

Gina 'The Veggie Goddess' Matthews, resides in sunny Phoenix, Arizona, and has been a lover of nature, gardening and, of course, vegetarian and vegan cuisine since childhood. 'The Veggie Goddess' strongly encourages home gardening, supporting your local farmers and organic food co-ops, animal rights, and sustaining and preserving the well-being of Mother Earth.

Printed in Great Britain
by Amazon